CRAFT TOPICS

MAPS AND MAPMAKING

FACTS ● THINGS TO MAKE ● ACTIVITIES

ANITA GANERI
Illustrated by Raymond Turvey

Franklin Watts
A Division of Grolier Publishing
New York ● London ● Hong Kong ● Sydney
Danbury, Connecticut

WARNING
You will need a sharp knife for some
of the projects in this book. Ask an
adult to help you and be very careful.
Always cut on a board when you are
using a knife or a saw.

© 1995 Franklin Watts

Franklin Watts
95 Madison Ave
New York, NY 10016

Editor: Annabel Martin
Designed by: Sally Boothroyd
Photography by: Martyn Chillmaid
Additional picture research by: Veneta Bullen
Consultant: Olive Pearson

Library of Congress Cataloging-in-Publication Data

Ganeri, Anita, 1961 –
    Maps and mapmaking / Anita Ganeri.
        p.   cm. – (Craft Topics)
    Includes index.
    ISBN 0-531-14370-8
    1. Cartography–Juvenile literature.   [1. Cartography.
    2. Handicraft.]   I. Title.   II. Title: Maps and mapmaking.
    III. Series.
    GA105.6.G36   1995
    912–dc20   94-40036
                                                    CIP AC

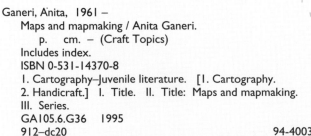

CURR
GA
105.6
.G36
1995

Printed in the United Kingdom

CONTENTS

WHAT IS A MAP?

A map is a picture of the world around us. There are many different types of map. One map might show the streets and landmarks in our local town. Another might show what the landscape is like for a whole country. Another might show the weather forecast for a whole continent.

STREET PLANS

A street plan is a map of the streets and buildings in a town or city. It shows the names of the streets, the names of different parts of the city, and railroad and bus stations. Street maps also show the important buildings that people might want to find, such as the library or police station.

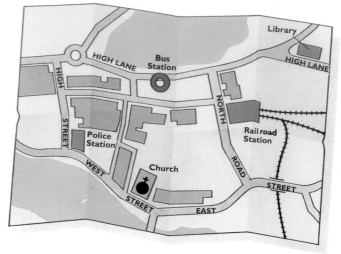

Street plan

BOOK OF MAPS

An atlas is a book of maps. A world atlas contains topographic maps of every country in the world, showing towns and cities, rivers and mountains, major roads, and railroads. It might also contain thematic maps, showing other things about the countries, such as what the climate is like or what crops are grown.

Atlas showing physical map (below)

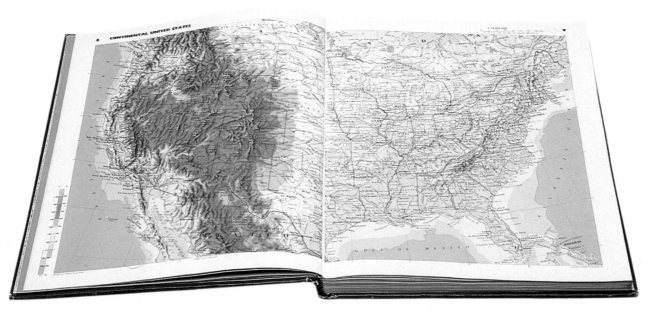

SPECIAL MAPS

Not all maps show areas of Earth's surface. There are many special types of map. For example, oceanographers use maps of the sea bottom; geologists use maps of the rocks under the ground; and astronomers use maps of the night sky and of the Moon.

MAKING MAPS

Making and studying maps is called cartography. To make a map, you need information about where things are and how big they are. For maps of small areas like your school, things can be measured and drawn by hand. Maps of large areas contain a huge amount of information. Measurements are taken from photographs and satellite images and stored on a computer.

Moon map (above)

Satellite image of Earth (below)

MAKING PLANS

A plan is a map of quite a small area, such as a room, a school, a shopping center, or the streets of a town center. A plan shows where things are so it is easy to find them.

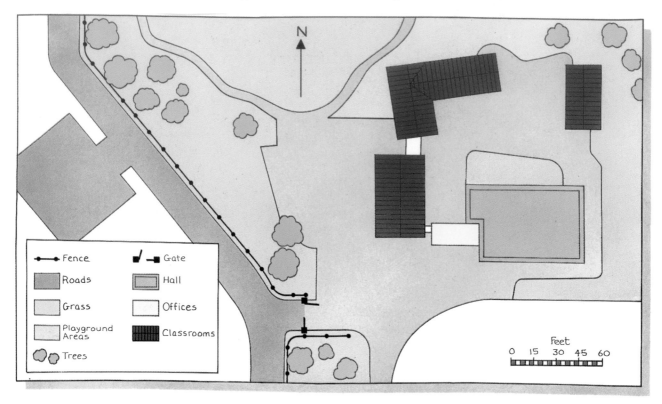

SYMBOLS AND KEYS

Different buildings and types of ground are shown on the plan in different colors. Objects such as trees and fences are shown by small pictures or shapes, which are called symbols. A person using the plan needs to know what the colors, lines and symbols mean, so a plan or map always has a key.

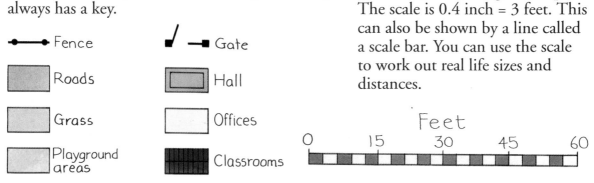

SCALE

Plans and maps are much smaller than the actual objects, areas, and distances that they show. In the plan shown here, an object 3 feet (1 m) long in real life is drawn .04 inch (1 mm) long on the plan. The scale is 0.4 inch = 3 feet. This can also be shown by a line called a scale bar. You can use the scale to work out real life sizes and distances.

DRAWING A PLAN

Try making a simple plan of your classroom or bedroom. You need to collect the information, decide what scale to use, then draw the plan. Finally, add a key and draw the scale on.

You will need: ● graph paper ● a pencil ● colored cardboard ● a tape measure ● a ruler ● colored pencils or pens

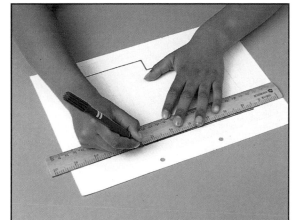

▲ **1.** Start by measuring the sides of your room. Now decide what scale to use. Try 2 inches (5 cm) on the plan for each 3 feet (1m or 100cm) in the room. So if one side of the room is 13 feet (4 m or 400 cm) long, it will be 8 inches (20 cm) long on the plan (13/8). Draw the sides of the room on your paper.

Try making colored shapes for the objects. Draw a plan of each object to scale and cut it out. Now you can use the plan to try fitting the things into your room in a different way.

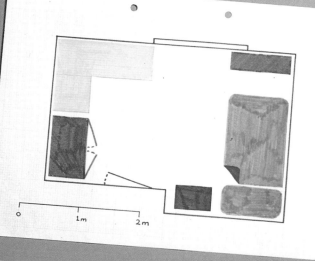

▲ **2.** Now measure the position and size of the bed, table, and dresser in your room. Draw them on the plan in the correct scale.

SYMBOLS AND SIZES

The information on a map is shown by lines, colors, and symbols. Symbols are small pictures or shapes that show small things on the ground, such as trees, churches, electricity towers, and so on. The meaning of all the symbols is shown in the key. Most maps also have a scale so that you can figure out distances from the map. A grid helps you to find places on the map quickly.

ROADS AND RAILROADS

Roads are shown as lines. Different colors are used for different types of road – one color for highways, another for main roads, and another for minor roads.

━━━━━━ Main Road

═══════ Minor Road

BUILDINGS

Buildings are shown as blocks of color. Important buildings such as churches, hospitals, and government buildings are shown with small symbols or letters.

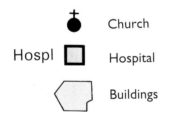

☩ Church

Hospl ☐ Hospital

⬡ Buildings

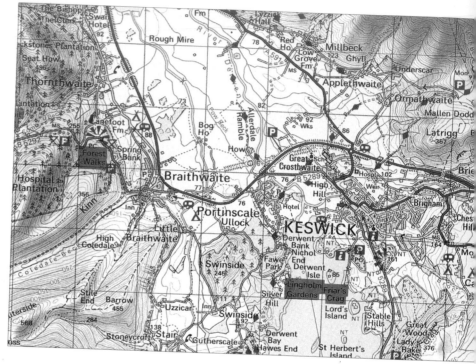

HOW FAR?

Maps of small areas that have a lot of detail, such as town plans, are called large-scale maps. Maps of large areas with less detail, such as maps of a country, are called small-scale maps. Every map has a scale so that you can figure out how far it is from one place to another on the map.

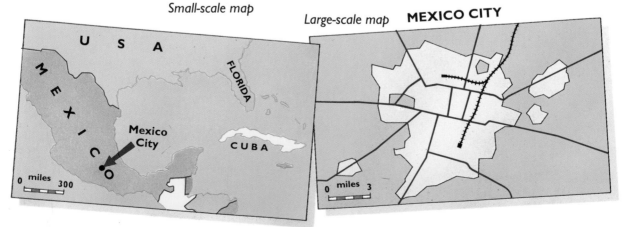

Small-scale map

Large-scale map **MEXICO CITY**

0 miles 300

0 miles 3

NATURAL FEATURES

Symbols and colors show what the ground is like. Tree symbols show woods. Blue lines show streams and rivers. The way the ground goes up and down to make hills and valleys is shown by shading or lines called contour lines. Contour lines are imaginary lines that join points that are the same height above sea level.

Rivers

Woodland

WHERE ON THE MAP?

A grid system is used to help find places on a map. Some maps use a simple grid with letters and numbers. Others use a grid like a graph. An accurate position can be given by saying how far across and up the map the point is. You can find out how to use grids on page 25.

You can find out how to use grids on page 25.

STRING MEASURER

You will need: ● string ● colored pens

You can measure distances on a map very easily using a piece of string.

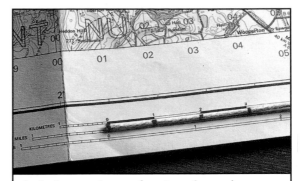

▲ 1. Lay a piece of string along the scale line on the map with one end of the string at the zero mark on the scale. At each division on the scale, make a mark on the string. Use different colors for large and small divisions.

2. To find the distance between two places, lay the string along the roads that you would have to go along. Count the divisions along the string to find the distance.

You can use the string measurer with any map that has the same scale.

9

MAKING MAPS

A map is made in two parts. First, all of the information needed (called data) is gathered together. The data is made up of measurements and other information, for example, what buildings are used for, what sorts of trees are in a wooded area, or where the ground is swampy. Only when all the data is collected can the map be drawn.

MEASURING THE GROUND

The data for large-scale, local maps and plans is gathered by measuring the ground. A surveyor starts at one point (such as a gatepost or the corner of a building) and measures the position of other points from it. For small, simple plans, the surveyor needs only a tape measure. For plans and maps of larger areas, special instruments are used. A theodolite is used to measure angles accurately. Electronic measuring devices use an infrared light beam to measure distances accurately.

PHOTOGRAPHY FROM THE SKY

The data for small-scale maps comes from photographs taken from airplanes or space satellites. The photographs are taken from above the area to be mapped. They are called aerial photographs. Lots of photographs are needed to cover a large area. The size and position of things can be measured from the photographs once they have been adjusted to account for distortions. Photographs also show what the land is being used for. Special satellite photographs can show up details of different types of vegetation on the ground.

Light aircraft taking overlapping photos (below)

STEREOSCOPIC VIEWING

If two photographs are taken from slightly different positions and looked at in a special viewer, the landscape can be seen in three dimensions. Hills and tall buildings seem to leap out of the picture. These photographs are called stereo photographs or stereo pairs. They are used to measure distances, sizes, and the height of the land.

Look at the pictures through two cardboard tubes — one for each eye. The pictures will merge to give a 3-D effect.

DRAWING A MAP

Once all the information has been gathered, the map can be drawn. Maps and plans used to be drawn in pen and ink but today it can also be done by computer. The computer uses data stored in it to draw different types of maps, such as a street plan, road map, or map of places to visit.

Information from a map being added into the map computer.

MAKE A TREASURE MAP

Imagine a tropical island with sandy beaches, swaying palm trees, thick forests, and high mountains. And imagine that somewhere on the island you have hidden a fortune in buried treasure. When you have a picture of the island in your head, you can make a map of the island, to show where the treasure is buried. Look at a map of a real island for ideas. Here's one way of making the map.

You will need: ● plain paper ● a pencil ● colored pens or pencils ● glue ● thin cardboard ● scissors ● a ruler ● Scotch tape

1. You can make your map as large or small as you like. The one shown here is about 16 inches x 24 inches (40 cm x 60 cm). It was made by joining four sheets of typewriter paper with Scotch tape.

▲ **2.** Before you start drawing, decide the scale of the map. This map uses a scale of 4 inches (10 cm) on the map for each mile (kilometer) on the island. Draw a grid on your map with lines every ¹/₄ mile (0.4 km).

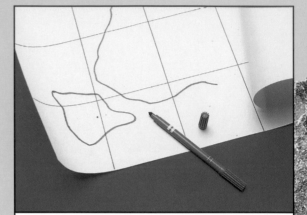

▲ **3.** In pencil, sketch the coastline of your island on the paper. Also sketch rocks and coral reefs in the sea. When you have finalized the shape, draw the coastline in blue pen.

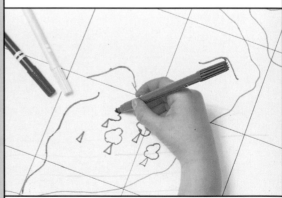

▲ **4.** Now decide where to put hills and mountains, rivers, lakes, forests, beaches, and cliffs. Design picture symbols for all these features and sketch them on your map in pencil. When you are happy with them, color them in.

5. Finish your map by adding a key to the symbols you have used. Remember to draw a scale as well. Fold the map carefully.

6. Finally, make a case for your map. Cut one piece of cardboard slightly bigger than the folded map. Cut another piece slightly bigger than the first. Fold the edges of the second piece around the edges of the first and glue them down. Decorate the case.

MOUNTAINS
RIVERS
LAKES
FOOTPATHS
TREES
PALM TREES
BEACH
CLIFFS
BURIED TREASURE

0   ½   1
km

MAP HISTORY

Today the whole world has been measured and mapped. However, just a hundred years ago many places were still unmapped. Five hundred years ago, European maps of the world did not show the Americas or Australia because the mapmakers did not know they existed.

THE FIRST MAPS

The oldest map we know of was made in about 2300 B.C. in Mesopotamia, which is now part of Iraq. The map was carved in a block of clay. The Egyptians and Greeks made maps of the parts of the world they knew about. In about A.D. 150, a Greek geographer named Ptolemy wrote down all he knew about maps and mapmaking in an eight-volume work-book called *Geography*.

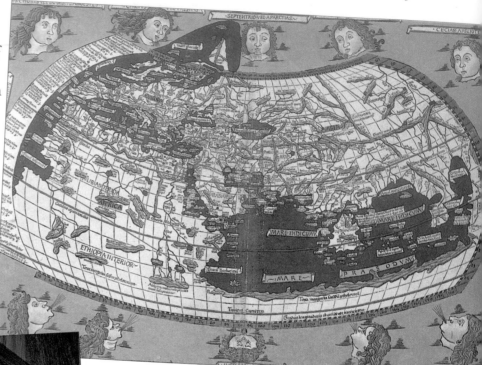

A map of the world according to Ptolemy (above)

IMAGINARY MAPS

Unfortunately, mapmaking got worse until the late 1400s. Medieval map-makers drew what they imagined the world looked like. They drew the Earth as a round shape, but they did not know what it was really like. The countries and continents were the wrong shapes and in the wrong places. Some maps showed the world surrounded by a huge river called Oceanus. However, in China and the Arab world, mapmaking improved during A.D. 800 and 1200.

This map of the world is called the Mappa Mundi. It was drawn in the 13th century.

14

BETTER MAPS

Maps started to get more realistic and more accurate in the 1400s. Explorers and traders began to travel across the oceans, finding new routes and new lands. They had just started to use the compass, so they could work out where they were and they made maps of the coastlines they found. When the explorers returned home the new information was added to maps. The invention of the printing press meant that maps could be copied more easily than when they had been drawn by hand. By 1800, there were accurate instruments for working out a ship's position on Earth's surface. People began to make accurate maps of land regions as well as coasts.

MAPS FROM THE AIR

Soon after the first airplane flew, in 1903, mapmakers started taking photographs of the ground below. This made mapmaking much quicker and more accurate. Most modern maps have been made using information from aerial photographs. The latest development in mapmaking is the use of computers to store all the information needed to draw a map.

MAPPING THE WORLD

The earth is shaped like a slightly squashed sphere. Making a map of the earth is difficult because you cannot draw the surface of the earth on a piece of paper without some areas of the earth being out of shape on the map.

THE POLES AND EQUATOR

Earth spins around an imaginary line called its axis. The points on Earth's surface at each end of the axis are called the North Pole and the South Pole. The imaginary line around the middle of Earth, halfway between the poles, is called the equator. The equator divides Earth into two parts, called the Northern Hemisphere and the Southern Hemisphere.

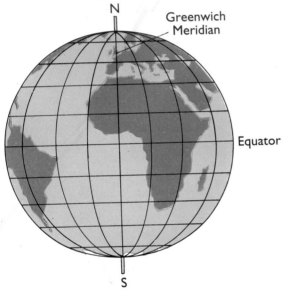

LATITUDE AND LONGITUDE

The position of a place on Earth's surface is measured by its latitude and longitude. Latitude and longitude are measured in angles, not in miles or kilometers. Longitude is a measure of how far around Earth a place is (starting from Greenwich in England and going to the east or to the west). Latitude is a measure of how far north or south of the equator the place is. The angles are measured from Earth's center. A map has lines on it showing the degrees of latitude and longitude.

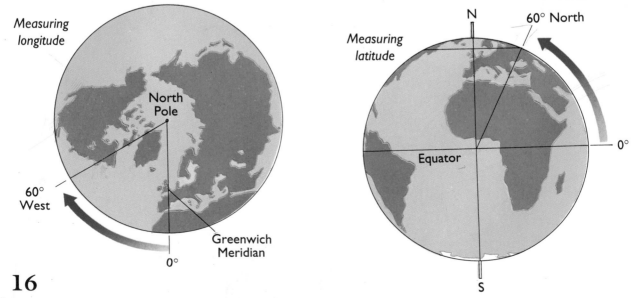

MAP PROJECTIONS

To draw a map of the world, you have to imagine Earth's surface unfolded and laid out flat (a bit like peeling an orange). This is called a map projection. There are many different types of map projections. Each one makes the countries look slightly different in shape and size.

A Mercator projection is used for sea charts. It makes the lines of latitude and longitude straight on the map, but the farther north and south you go, the more stretched and distorted the map gets. Greenland looks much bigger than it really is.

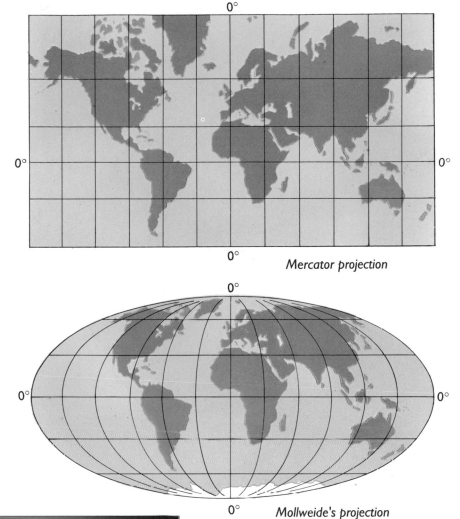

Mercator projection

Mollweide's projection

Mollweide's projection makes the countries look the right size compared with each other. Remember that the areas on the far left and far right are actually next to each other in real life.

GLOBES

A globe is a map of the world drawn on a sphere. A globe is the only sort of map that shows the countries and continents in their correct place and the right size and shape. You can find out about globes on pages 18-19.

MAKE A PAPER GLOBE

A globe is the only sort of map that can show the whole world with all the countries in their correct position and the right shape and size. Here's how to make a globe from paper.

You will need: ● tracing paper ● glue ● thin cardboard ● scissors ● paper ● thick cardboard ● a black pen ● a ruler ● colored pens or pencils ● drawing pins ● thin wooden dowel

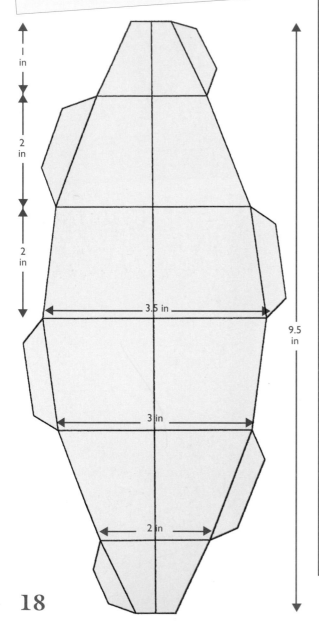

1 in

2 in

2 in

3.5 in

3 in

2 in

9.5 in

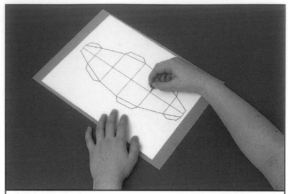

▲ **1.** Copy the template on the left onto tracing paper. Lay the tracing paper on a piece of thin cardboard. Push a drawing pin through the tracing paper to make marks in the thin cardboard where the lines on the template start and finish.

2. In pencil, join the holes you have made to produce a copy of the template. Make six copies in total. Draw over all the lines with a black pen and cut out the shapes. Using a ruler and the point of a pair of scissors, score along the lines.

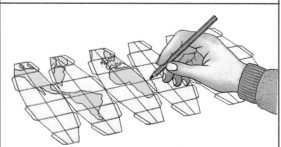

▲ **3.** Lay the six shapes side by side. Now copy the world map shown on the right onto the shapes. Use the lines on the map and the shapes to help you get the countries in the right places.

18

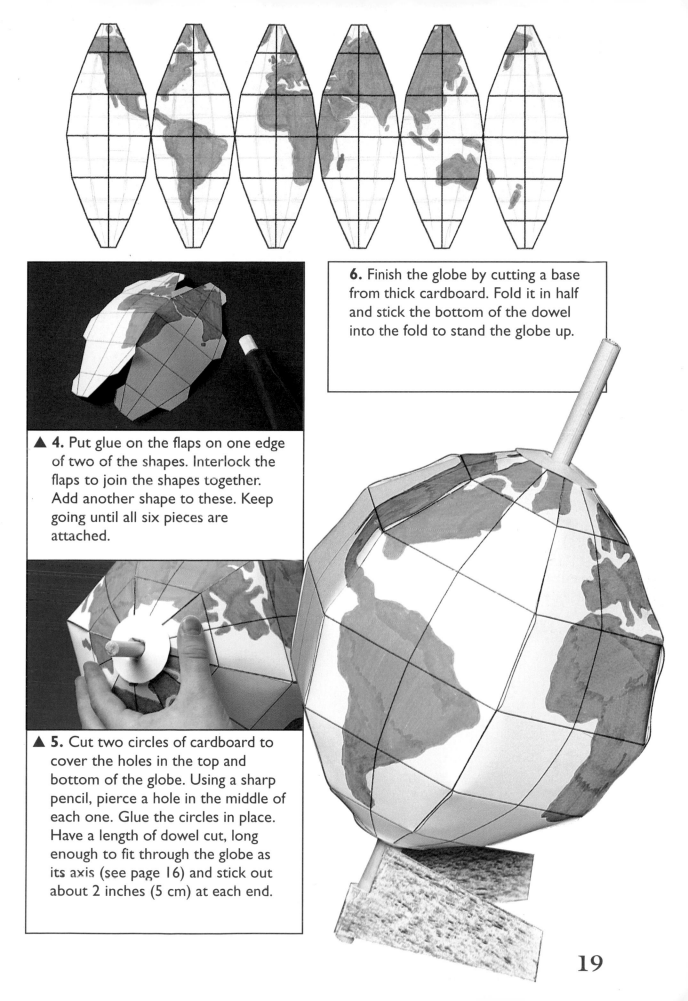

6. Finish the globe by cutting a base from thick cardboard. Fold it in half and stick the bottom of the dowel into the fold to stand the globe up.

▲ **4.** Put glue on the flaps on one edge of two of the shapes. Interlock the flaps to join the shapes together. Add another shape to these. Keep going until all six pieces are attached.

▲ **5.** Cut two circles of cardboard to cover the holes in the top and bottom of the globe. Using a sharp pencil, pierce a hole in the middle of each one. Glue the circles in place. Have a length of dowel cut, long enough to fit through the globe as its axis (see page 16) and stick out about 2 inches (5 cm) at each end.

19

INFORMATION ON MAPS

A particular area can have many different types of maps. For example, a map of Europe could show the borders between the different countries, the road and railroad network, the crops that are grown in each country, or what the landscape is like.

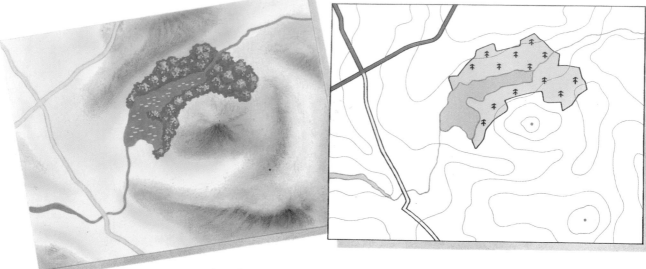

Relief map

Contour map

PHYSICAL MAPS

A physical map shows what the landscape is like. It shows hills and mountains, rivers and lakes, forests and deserts. Contour lines are used to show how the land rises and falls in hills, mountains, and valleys. Each line connects places of the same height. On some maps the areas between the contours are shaded. Many physical maps also show the manmade features on the landscape, such as towns, roads, and railroads.

POLITICAL MAPS

A political map shows how the world is divided up into countries or regions. For example, a political map of the world shows the outline of every country of the world. The countries can be shaded in different colors. It might also show the capital city of each country.

Political map of Europe (right)

CLIMATE

The climate of a place describes what the weather is normally like there during the year. For example, the climate in western Europe is warm and dry in the summer and cold and wet in the winter. Climate maps normally show the average rainfall and average temperature during January and July.

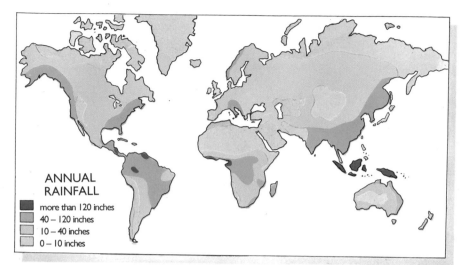

ANNUAL RAINFALL
- more than 120 inches
- 40 – 120 inches
- 10 – 40 inches
- 0 – 10 inches

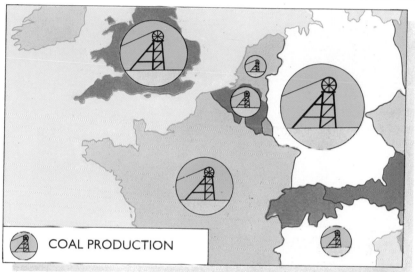

COAL PRODUCTION

Rainfall map (above)
Coal resource map (left)

RESOURCES MAP

A resources map shows what sort of agricultural or natural resources, such as crops or minerals, there are in a certain area. The amount of a resource is shown by a picture symbol. The bigger the symbol, or the more the symbol appears, the more of the resource there is.

ROAD MAP

A road map is designed to make finding a route as easy as possible. The roads are brightly colored and clearly numbered. Because road maps are often used by tourists, places of interest, such as monuments and battlefields, are shown by special symbols.

MAKE A 3-D RELIEF MAP

You can make a contour map that is actually shaped like the landscape. After building up the shape, you can paint on features such as forest and rivers.

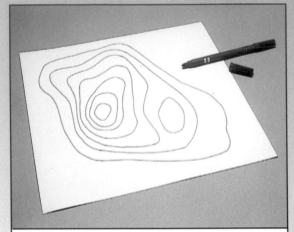

You will need: ● a craft knife ● a pencil ● newspaper ● plain white paper ● paints ● thick cardboard about 12 inches square (about 30 cm square) ● corrugated cardboard or old Styrofoam tiles ● brushes ● scissors ● wallpaper paste (fungicide free)

▲ **1.** Start with a sheet of plain paper 8½ x 11 in (21 x 28 cm). Design hills and valleys by drawing contour lines on the paper. Start with contours to represent low heights and work up to the tops of the hills.

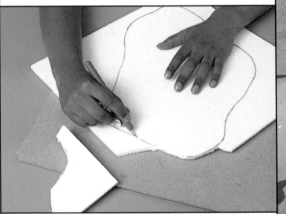

▲ **2.** Cut around the lowest contour on your map. Lay the shape on a piece of Styrofoam and draw around it. Carefully using a craft knife, cut the shape out of the cardboard.

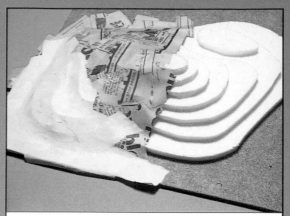

▲ **3.** Stick the Styrofoam shape onto thick cardboard. Now cut around the next contour line on your contour map and use it to make another Styrofoam shape. Stick this on top of the first layer of Styrofoam. Continue until every layer is finished.

▲ **4.** Cover the layers of Styrofoam with strips of newspaper soaked in wallpaper paste. Keep adding paper until you have built up two or three layers. Finish with a layer of plain white paper.

5. When the paper has dried out, you can start painting the relief map. Use colors to show the different sorts of ground, such as fields, forests, and hilltops. Paint in streams and lakes. Add roads and buildings if you want.

USING MAPS

You can use a map to find your way from place to place or to look up information about the landscape around you. Before you can plan a route, you need to work out your position on the map, then match the directions on the map with the directions on the ground.

FINDING YOUR PLACE

To find your position on the map, look for a landmark such as a church or a road junction. Then match the real landmark with the landmark on the map. Study the map and check that it matches the other features around you.

WHICH WAY?

Once you know where you are, you need to work out which direction you are looking in and turn the map around so it matches the ground. This is called orientating the map. This is quite easy if you are on a road or path. However, if you are in the countryside you would need to use a compass if there were no landmarks. Turn the map until the symbol on the map, which shows magnetic north, lines up with the compass needle. Now the directions on the map are the same as in real life.

HOW FAR?

You can work out how far it is along a route from one place to another by looking at the scale. Use a map measurer like the one on page 9 to work out the distance accurately, or just make a rough estimate. Road maps show the distances between large towns or cities and major road junctions with numbers written next to the road.

USING THE GRID

The position of a landmark can be given by using the grid on a map. The index of an atlas or street plan gives the position of towns and cities by indicating which page and grid square it is on. On maps that have a grid with letters and numbers, positions are given by the letter first, then the number. This is called a grid reference. Other maps have a grid with latitude and longitude numbers marked, like a graph. Here a position can be given by specifying the latitude and longitude numbers of the point.

SPECIAL MAPS

Most maps show the surface of Earth. However, there are many other sorts of maps. There are maps for special uses, such as navigating at sea, and maps of special places, such as the bottom of the oceans and the surface of the moon.

CHARTS

A chart is a map used for navigation. Marine charts are used on board ships. Marine charts show the position of lighthouses, buoys, and wrecks, plus other navigational information. They also show the depth of the water and the position of dangerous sandbars so that a ship can avoid going aground. The grid on a chart is made up of lines of latitude and longitude. The scale shows nautical miles, which are the unit of distance used at sea. One nautical mile equals 1.25 miles (1.8 km) on the ground. Aeronautical charts are used by pilots. They show airport details, radio beacons, and navigational information.

MAPS FOR ASTRONOMERS

Astronomers use maps showing the position of the stars and constellations (groups of stars). These maps are called star charts. Star charts are a bit like maps of Earth. Some parts have to be stretched to fit the chart on a flat piece of paper. The only way to show the stars properly is by drawing the chart onto the inside of a sphere.

A planetarium shows stars by projecting a chart onto the inside of a large dome.

OCEANOGRAPHIC CHARTS

An oceanographic chart is a relief map of the bottom of the seas and oceans. Scientists use sound-measuring instruments called sonar to measure the depth of the sea. The sonar sends a pulse of sound down into the sea. The sound bounces off the seabed and back again. The deeper the sea, the longer the sound takes to get back up to the ship.

COMPUTERIZED MAPS

Road map software can be used to make a computer calculate the best route between two places. The computer stores information about all the roads and how they connect together. It can work out the shortest route or the fastest route and then print directions for a motorist to use on a journey.

SHINING STAR MAP

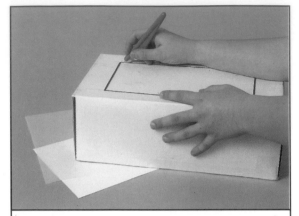

You will need: ● cardboard box ● scissors ● a craft knife ● pins ● tracing paper ● thin cardboard ● a star chart ● tape

3. Put the star chart tracing over the thin cardboard. Make a tiny hole for each star by pushing a pin through the tracing paper and the cardboard. Finally, stick the cardboard over the second hole in the box. Hold the box up to the light to see the star chart.

▲ **1.** Tape down any loose flaps on the cardboard box. Using a craft knife, carefully cut two holes in opposite sides of the box. Cut a piece of tracing paper large enough to cover one of the holes, and tape it in place. Cut a piece of thin cardboard large enough to cover the other hole.

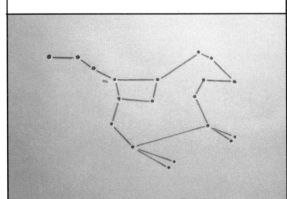

2. Lay tracing paper over the star chart and trace the positions of some of the star constellations.

ROAD MAPS

Many maps show things on the ground in their right places and at the correct size in relationship to each other. Sometimes, however, such details are not important. For example, a map showing railroad routes between towns and cities does not need to show the bends in the railroad track. It just needs to show how the towns are connected. This sort of map is called a road map.

Another example of a road map is a highway map. When you are in a car on a highway, you do not need to know how it twists and turns. You just need to know where to turn off, so a highway map can be drawn with straight lines.

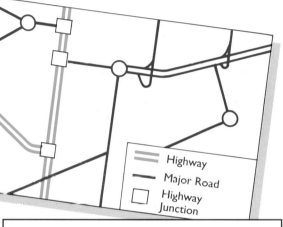

Highway
Major Road
Highway Junction

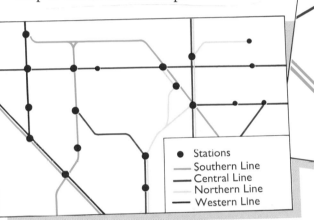

● Stations
Southern Line
Central Line
Northern Line
Western Line

WOOLY ROAD MAP

You will need: ● colored wool yarns
● drawing pins ● a road map
● plywood

1. Look at the road map. Mark each big town or large road junction by pushing a drawing pin into the plywood. Use a different colored wool for each type of road (highways, major and minor roads). Tie the strands of wool around the drawing pins to connect the big towns and junctions.

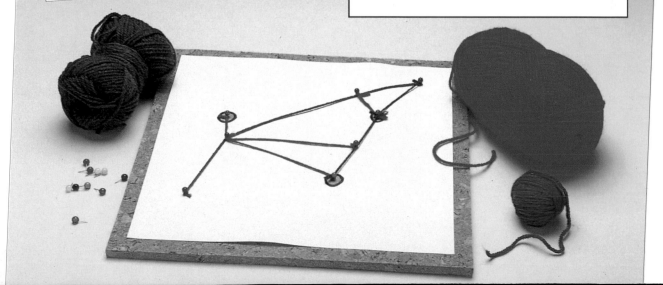

GLOSSARY

Chart – A special type of map used for navigation. Marine charts are used by sailors, and aeronautical charts are used by pilots.

Contour – A line on a contour map that connects points of equal height above mean sea level (see below).

Equator – An imaginary line around the middle of Earth.

Hemisphere – Half of a sphere. For map-making purposes, we imagine Earth is divided into two hemispheres (the Southern Hemisphere and the Northern Hemisphere) by the equator.

Key – A list on a map, showing what the symbols on the map mean.

Latitude – The position of a point on Earth, measured in degrees north or south from the equator.

Longitude – The position of a point on Earth, measured in degrees east or west from an imaginary line between the poles running through Greenwich, England.

Magnetic north – The point on Earth's surface toward which the north pole of a magnet points if allowed to swing freely.

Mean sea level – The average level of the sea during the year. Mean sea level is used as a base when measuring the height of points on land.

Oceanography – The study of the sea.

Plan – A large-scale map of a small area of land.

Poles – The two points (called the North Pole and South Pole) at each end of Earth's axis.

Political map – A map showing political information, such as the boundaries between countries and capital cities.

Projection – A way of showing the curved surface of the earth on a flat sheet of paper.

Relief map – A map showing how the land rises and falls in hills and valleys.

Road map – A map showing how places are linked together, for example, by roads or railroads.

Scale – The size of objects on a map compared with their actual size.

Theodolite – A device used by surveyors to measure angles very accurately.

Topographic map – A map showing the physical features (natural and manmade) on the earth's surface, such as roads, rivers, lakes, and buildings.

RESOURCES

MATERIALS
Most of the items used in the projects in this book can be obtained from craft shops, artists' supply stores or large stationery stores.

PLACES TO VISIT
The places listed below have exhibitions related to maps, or collections of maps. In addition, most local museums and libraries will have maps of the local area, as well as national and international maps and atlases. To find out where your local museums are, contact your local tourist information center or look in the telephone directory.

Book stores also have maps.
Rand McNally has its own store.

Rand McNally Map and Travel Store
150 East 52nd Street
New York
NY10022
(212) 758-7488

BOOKS TO READ

Baynes, John. *How Maps Are Made*. New York: Facts on File, 1989.

Lye, Keith. *Measuring and Maps*. New York: Gloucester Press, 1991.

Morris, Scott. *How to Read a Map*. New York: Chelsea House, 1993.

Porter, Malcolm. *The Dillon Press Children's Atlas*. New York: Macmillan Childrens Group, 1993.

Stefoff, Rebecca. *The Young Oxford Companion to Maps and Mapmaking*. New York: Oxford University Press, 1994.

Most children's atlases will contain information about maps. Look in your local library.

Additional photographs:

Ancient Art & Architecture Collection 14 (both); Eye Ubiquitous © Gavin Wickham 15; Robert Harding Picture Library 26 (t); Angelo Hornack 11(both); The London Planetarium 26 (b); Portfolio Pictures 5; Tony Stone Images © Dan Bosler 21; ZEFA 17.